W9-AMO-017

Inventions and Discoveries

# Industry and Manufacturing

**WORLD BOOK**

a Scott Fetzer company

Chicago

**www.worldbookonline.com**

World Book, Inc.
233 N. Michigan Avenue
Chicago, IL 60601
U.S.A.

For information about other World Book publications, visit our Web site at **http://www.worldbookonline.com** or call **1-800-WORLDBK (967-5325).**
For information about sales to schools and libraries, call **1-800-975-3250 (United States),** or **1-800-837-5365 (Canada).**

**Editorial:**

**Editor in Chief:** Paul A. Kobasa
**Project Manager:** Cassie Mayer
**Editor:** Brian Johnson
**Content Development:** Odyssey Books
**Writer:** Rebecca McEwen
**Researchers:** Cheryl Graham, Jacqueline Jasek
**Manager, Contracts & Compliance**
  **(Rights & Permissions):** Loranne K. Shields
**Indexer:** David Pofelski

**Graphics and Design:**

**Associate Director:** Sandra M. Dyrlund
**Manager:** Tom Evans
**Coordinator, Design Development and Production:**
 Brenda B. Tropinski
**Senior Designer:** Don Di Sante
**Contributing Photographs Editor:** Clover Morell
**Senior Cartographer:** John M. Rejba

**Pre-Press and Manufacturing:**

**Director:** Carma Fazio
**Manufacturing Manager:** Steven K. Hueppchen
**Production/Technology Manager:** Anne Fritzinger

**Picture Acknowledgments:**

Front Cover: Digital Vision/SuperStock; Back Cover: © North Wind Picture Archives.

© Alan King engraving/Alamy Images 19; © Caro/Alamy Images 13; © Phil Degginger, Alamy Images 38; © Mark Dyball, Alamy Images 27; © Mary Evans Picture Library/Alamy Images 6, 17; © Niall McDiarmid, Alamy Images 8; © The Print Collector/Alamy Images 17, 26, 34; © Steve Bloom Images/Alamy Images 5; © Vintage Images/Alamy Images 20; © Rob Walls, Alamy Images 13; © Wendy White, Alamy Images 7; © World History Archive/Alamy Images 11; © Konrad Zelazowski, Alamy Images 26; AP/Wide World 5, 33, 35, 36, 39, 41, 43; © Getty Images 22; © AFP/Getty Images 33; © Daniel Berehulak, Getty Images 11; © Gregory A. Harlin, National Geographic/Getty Images 4; © Hulton Archive/Getty Images 24, 30, 31, 32, 44; © Louie Psihoyos, Science Faction/Getty Images 39; © Jeff Shaffer/Dawn Smith, StockFood Creative/Getty Images 29; Granger Collection 19, 21, 42; © Amit Dave, Reuters/Landov 25; © Seokyong Lee, Bloomberg News/Landov 6; © Lucas Schifres, Bloomberg News/Landov 40; NASA/JPL 41; © North Wind Pictures 25; © Eurelios/Photo Researchers 39; Shutterstock 9, 10, 12, 13, 14, 15, 18, 23, 28, 29, 36, 37, 44; © Alex Wilson, West Virginia Development Office 16.

All maps and illustrations are the exclusive property of World Book, Inc.

**Library of Congress Cataloging-in-Publication Data**

Industry and manufacturing.
     p. cm. – (Inventions and discoveries)
  Summary: "An exploration of the transformative impact of inventions and discoveries in industry and manufacturing. Features include fact boxes, sidebars, biographies, timeline, glossary, list of recommended reading and Web sites, and index"–Provided by publisher.
  Includes index.
  ISBN 978-0-7166-0389-4
  1. Discoveries in science–Social aspects–Juvenile literature. 2. Inventions–Juvenile literature.
I. World Book, Inc.
Q180.55.D571344 2009
609–dc22
                                          2008045601

Inventions and Discoveries
Set ISBN: 978-0-7166-0380-1
Printed in China
1 2 3 4 5 12 11 10 09

# Table of Contents

There is a glossary of terms on pages 45-46. Terms defined in the glossary are in type **that looks like this** on their first appearance on any spread (two facing pages).

# ► Introduction

In ancient times, people melted such metals as copper over a fire and shaped them into tools.

## What are industry and manufacturing?

**Industry** is any branch of business, trade, or manufacture (the making of goods). Large businesses manufacture many different tools and products.

Since prehistoric times, human beings have created tools that would help them to survive, help them do work, or make their lives easier or more pleasant. About 2.6 million years ago, they shaped tools out of stone. They learned that some kinds of stone are better than others for making tools. They invented new kinds of tools to do certain jobs.

As prehistoric people met new challenges to their survival, they invented new technology to help them survive and succeed. These inventions form a line stretching from the first people living on grasslands millions of years ago to the busy people living in modern cities today.

Many of the tools we use today are incredibly complicated. For this reason and others, people no longer make most of their own tools. Instead, businesses manufacture tools and the other products that people need.

## What is an invention?

An invention is a new device, new product, or new way of doing something. Before the car was invented, some people rode horses to travel long distances. Before the light bulb was invented, people used candles and similar sources of light to see at night. Almost 2 million years ago, the creation of the spear and the bow and arrow helped people hunt better. Today, inventions continue to change the way people live.

Today, there are thousands of industries. They grow our food, construct our buildings, and provide our entertainment. The rise of industry has meant rapid growth in the variety of products and services that are available to modern people. Such products and services have also become much less expensive.

Industries have changed dramatically over the centuries, and they are certain to change further in coming years. Through thousands of years of invention and change, industry has built the modern world.

Today, large factories make most of the goods found in stores.

# Fire

Factories burn fuel to melt metals in furnaces.

For many thousands of years, people have used fire to keep warm and to cook food. Our ancestors may have built fires as long as 2 million years ago. Certainly, by half a million years ago, people had mastered the art of building and controlling fires. As time passed, people invented new ways to use fire. They learned that fire could help them shape or improve weapons and other tools. They discovered that fire could be used to bake soft clay into hard pottery.

As people studied fire, they learned that different kinds of fuel change how fire can be used. For example, burning coal gives off heat but it does not create much flame. As a result, people burned coal for heat rather than light. By contrast, burning gas or oil produces bright flames, so people used gas or oil to fuel lamps.

Until about 200 years ago, the only ways that people could make fire were through **friction** and by using flint (a hard rock) and metal. To use friction, a person whirled a stick in a notch in a board. As the stick spun against the

The Chinese have used fire to make pottery since ancient times.

board, it created a fine, powdery saw-dust. At the same time, friction heated the sawdust. When the sawdust got hot enough, it burst into flame. With the flint and metal method, a person made sparks by knocking a piece of flint against a piece of metal. These sparks could be used to start a fire.

It was relatively difficult and time-consuming to create fire using these methods. Often, people fed their fires a small but steady supply of fuel. This kept the fire lit even when it wasn't needed. This began to change in 1827. In that year, an English pharmacist named John Walker invented the first match. Matches made starting a fire easier and faster. Other improvements in matches quickly followed. By 1943, scientists had invented matches that would still light after eight hours underwater.

Learning to control fire was one of the most important discoveries ancient people made. With time, the impor-tance of fire has only grown. Today, fire is important to nearly every **industry.** Burning gasoline drives the engines in most cars. Most **power plants** burn coal or other fuels to create electric power. Factories use fire to melt metals out of **ore.** These metals can then be shaped into everything from jewelry to cooking pots. Fire shooting from the end of a rocket can even carry people into space.

Aboriginal tribes-men teach a young boy how to make a fire by using friction.

**F U N   F A C T**

Fighting fires is its own in-dustry. Two thousand years ago, the ancient **Romans** or-ganized groups of firefight-ers to put out fires before they could spread. More recently, Benjamin Franklin helped form the first volunteer fire company in America in 1736. He also organ-ized the Union Fire Company in Philadelphia, Pennsylvania, and made himself its first fire chief.

# Manufactured Glass

When glass is melted, it can be blown into hollow shapes, such as bottles.

Glass is one of the most useful materials in the world. People use glass in countless ways. They drink out of glass containers. They see through glass windows. They wear special glass lenses mounted in frames to correct their eyesight. People even use glass in jewelry and decoration.

Few of the things we manufacture add as much to modern living as glass.

However, glass is made from raw materials that are inexpensive and widespread. Most glass is made from such common materials as sand, soda ash, and limestone. These ingredients are mixed together and melted into a liquid. The liquid is blown or poured into particular shapes. When the liquid cools, it hardens into glass.

Although the raw materials needed to make glass are widespread, it took people a long time to learn how to make glass. Before people knew how to make glass, they used glass that they found in nature. For example, people collected dark volcanic glass called obsidian (ob SIHD ee uhn). They used obsidian to make jewelry and weapons. They even used it as a form of money.

People probably first made glass around 3000 B.C. The first glass that people could produce was a sort of glaze on ceramic pots. By 1500 B.C., people in Egypt and elsewhere in the Middle East were making the first glass containers. Soon, people began to make colored glass for jewelry, cosmetics cases, and tiny jars. Early glassmaking was slow and expensive. As a result,

Glass can be used to make cookware that tolerates high heat.

Long glass tubes carry information around the world at great speed.

few people could afford to buy glass, which could cost as much as jewels.

Around 30 B.C., people in the Middle East invented the blowpipe. Glassmakers use blowpipes to blow glass into a hollow bulb, which can then be shaped. This invention made glass production easier, faster, and cheaper. People began to use glass to store wine, honey, and oils. By A.D. 1200, people in Europe had perfected the art of making stained glass windows. In Venice, Italy, artists made delicate, beautiful glass decorations.

Eventually, people began to make glass in factories. By 1890, the glass **industry** was making so much glass at such low cost that it could be used for everything from food containers to light bulbs. Improvements in manufacturing made glass affordable to everyone.

Today, the glass industry makes glass pipelines, cookware, building blocks, and heat **insulation.** Glass is

even made into communication cables. Factories spin the glass into long tubes that are thinner than a human hair. Light travels along these **optical fibers** at tremendous speed, carrying information around the world.

**A CLOSER LOOK**

Glassmaking got off to a rough start in the colonies that later became the United States of America. In 1608, English colonists built the first glass factory in Jamestown, Virginia. However, disease, crop failures, and war with Native Americans killed off many of the people in Jamestown. The factory failed. In 1621, Jamestown colonists built another glass factory, but by 1624, this factory had failed, too. It wasn't until 1739 that colonists in New Jersey were able to build a glassmaking factory that succeeded.

Gears are wheels with teeth that mesh together.

The most important invention of all time is probably the wheel. Almost every kind of machine uses some sort of wheel. Prehistoric people learned to use smooth logs as wheels. Logs could be used to roll such heavy objects as stone blocks from place to place. By 3500 B.C., people in the Middle East had begun to build carts with simple wooden wheels. Such carts made it much easier to move goods over long distances.

Around 500 B.C., people discovered how to use wheels in a new way. They carved blocky teeth into wheels to make **gears.** Gears always work in pairs. The teeth in one gear match up with the teeth in another gear. When one gear is turned, it causes the other gear to turn, too. If the first gear turns to the right, the gear it meshes with will turn to the left. A spinning gear turns an **axle** that can be used to do work.

The earliest machines to use gears were quite simple. For example, one of the first ways people learned to provide power for **industry** was by using a **water wheel.** A water wheel was originally a large, wooden wheel that spun with the flow of a river. As the water wheel spun, it turned an axle that was connected to gears. These gears caused large stones to grind grain into flour. Water wheels provided power for factories long before people learned to use steam. In fact, grain **mills** powered by water wheels were the world's first factories.

Today, people have invented many different kinds of gears to accomplish different tasks. Gears are an important part of many modern machines, especially automobiles. In a car, the engine drives gears that power the wheels. Every time people drive down the road, they use ancient technology in their modern machines.

Water wheels use gears to power machinery from the 1500's.

An engineer adjusts the clock inside the Big Ben clock tower in London, England.

# Pulleys and Levers

Pulleys are used in cranes to lift heavy weights.

A basic pulley is just a wheel with a rope over the top of it. Pulleys are especially useful for lifting heavy objects. A person can hang a pulley above the object, attaching the object to one end of the rope. The person grabs the other end of the rope. When the person pulls down on the rope, the wheel changes the direction of this force so that it lifts the object on the other side.

The pulley is a useful tool because pulling down on a rope is much easier than trying to lift a heavy object directly. With a pulley, a person can use his or her body weight in addition to muscle strength.

People still use pulleys in many of the same ways they did in ancient times. Around 2,000 years ago, people used pulleys for such tasks as raising construction materials into place or lowering heavy things into a boat. Today, mechanical pulleys on cranes lift massive steel beams to the tops of **skyscrapers.** Modern cranes using pulleys can load hundreds of heavy containers onto a ship in a single day.

Pulleys are an important part of most engines. Pulleys with grooved

**G**ears were one of the first ways that people used wheels for more than simple transportation. However, the wheel has been adapted countless times since then. Around 400 B.C., the ancient Greeks invented the first **pulleys.**

A hammer can be used as a lever to pull nails.

wheels, connected by belts, carry force through an engine. As the engine turns one of the pulley's wheels, the wheel pulls the belt with it. The belt then turns a pulley wheel in another part of the engine.

A **lever** is another simple machine that was discovered thousands of years ago. A lever works by using a bar that rests on a **fulcrum,** the support on which a lever turns or is supported in moving or lifting something. A person can place one end of the bar under an object, such as a heavy rock, and set a fulcrum under the bar. When the person pushes down on the raised end of the bar, the fulcrum forces the other end of the bar to rise. This then lifts the object.

Like a pulley, a lever allows a person to use both muscle strength and body weight to move an object.

## A CLOSER LOOK

**Six Simple Machines**

1. Inclined plane (ramp): a structure used to raise heavy loads with relatively small forces.
2. Lever: a simple machine that can help lift a weight with less effort.
3. Pulley: a wheel over which a rope or belt is passed for the purpose of transmitting force and doing work.
4. Screw: an inclined plane wrapped in a spiral around a shaft.
5. Wedge: a simple machine that can be used to adjust the positions of heavy objects.
6. Wheel and **axle**: a mechanical device used in lifting loads.

Levers, such as this car jack, make it easier to lift heavy objects.

# ► Concrete

Concrete was one of the materials used to build the Pantheon in Rome, Italy. The building has stood for nearly 2,000 years.

Long ago, people built every structure they needed for their own family to survive. As cities grew and improvements in farming provided more food, people could focus on doing only one kind of work. This allowed them to become experts in that **industry.** Soon, workers trained for years to master all knowledge relating to their industry.

Over time, people invented new methods for constructing larger, more complex buildings. The invention of simple machines, such as **levers** and **pulleys,** allowed workers to move extremely heavy stones during construction. However, new construction materials were needed to improve buildings further. When people invented concrete, it forever changed the construction industry.

Concrete starts as a liquid mixture of cement, sand, gravel, crushed stone, and water. When concrete dries, it becomes as strong and durable as stone. Like stone, concrete resists fire and water, but concrete also offers many advantages over stone. For example, concrete can be poured where it is needed and made into a wide variety of shapes.

People in the Middle East began to use an early form of concrete no later than 3400 B.C. However, concrete did not meet its potential until the **Romans** began to use it in the 200's B.C. Soon, the Romans learned that mixing a kind of volcanic ash into their concrete made it even stronger. Such concrete could also harden underwater.

The Romans used their new concrete to construct buildings that once would have collapsed. For example,

Concrete is strong enough to hold back huge bodies of water.

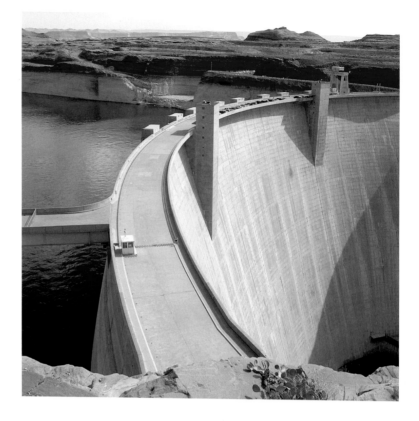

around A.D. 125, the Romans built a large temple called the Pantheon. The Pantheon featured a soaring concrete dome (curved roof) that was 142 feet (43 meters) across and weighed 5,000 tons (4,536 metric tons). The Pantheon was a triumph of Roman construction, and it remained the largest dome in the world for the next 1,300 years. Incredibly, the Pantheon still stands today, nearly 2,000 years after it was built.

The Romans used concrete to build roads, bridges, walls, and buildings. Like the Pantheon, some of these structures survive to this day. Unfortunately, when the western part of the Roman Empire fell in the A.D. 400's, people in Europe lost the art of making concrete.

It was not until 1756 that an English **engineer** named John Smeaton rediscovered how to make concrete. Since then, people have discovered ways to make concrete that is even stronger than the concrete the Romans used. Today, concrete remains one of the most useful building materials. The construction industry uses concrete to build roads, pipes, **skyscrapers,** and tunnels.

## A CLOSER LOOK

Some of the most massive construction projects on Earth have used concrete, and a lot of it. The Hoover Dam is the largest public construction project ever completed in the United States. It used 4.5 million cubic yards (3.4 million cubic meters) of concrete. That is enough concrete to pave a highway stretching from San Francisco, California, to New York City. The world's tallest building, the Burj Dubai (*duh BY*) in the United Arab Emirates, relies on reinforced concrete to rise to a height of more than 2,300 feet (700 meters).

# ► Coal

**Coal fueled the rise of modern industry.**

When the western part of the Roman Empire collapsed in the A.D. 400's, much European understanding of science and technology collapsed as well. For more than a thousand years in Europe, progress in the technology people used came at a relatively slow pace. In fact, some knowledge, such as the recipe for concrete, was lost for centuries. This period is often called the **Middle Ages. Industry** developed slowly during this time.

Eventually, a new period of discovery in science and the arts called the **Renaissance** swept through Europe. The Renaissance began in Italy in the 1300's and spread to other countries in the 1400's.

During this period, many new industries quickly arose. People improved and built new navigation tools for ships, which helped them map and explore the world. Trade (the buying and selling of goods) grew rapidly, and merchants (traders) started to bring exotic goods home from abroad. Scientists designed many new machines. Some new inventions produced entirely new industries.

One thing that all industries had in common was a need for power. Early industry used **water wheels** or **windmills** to provide power. However, water and wind power had their limitations. A windmill is useless when there is no wind, and water wheels require flowing water. People began to search for new sources of power.

Coal gradually became the most important source of power in Europe. Prehistoric people knew that coal could be burned for heat, and ancient people

late 1600's, an English minister named John Clayton burned coal and collected the gas in animal bladders. When he punctured the bladders, he found he could light on fire the escaping gas.

In 1792, a British **engineer** named William Murdock figured out how to light his home using gas he made from coal. By 1804, Murdock had installed hundreds of lamps that burned gas in English cotton mills. Within three years, the first gas lamps were installed on London's streets.

Coal could be used to heat buildings, turn water into steam, and light the streets of growing cities. By the late 1700's, coal was driving the most rapid growth in industry and manufacturing the world has ever known. This period, called the **Industrial Revolution,** began in England and soon spread to the rest of the world.

used coal to melt metals. It was not until the 1600's, however, that coal was widely used in Europe. At that time, a severe shortage of wood in western Europe caused people to switch to coal. Coal was especially plentiful in England. By the late 1600's, England produced about 80 percent of the world's coal.

In 1609, a Belgian chemist and doctor named Jan Baptista van Helmont discovered manufactured gas. When he heated coal, he realized that it gave off a "spirit." He called this spirit "gas." In the

Gas made from coal lighted London's streets in the 1800's.

# ▶ The Steam Engine

**Steam engines revolutionized transportation.**

In the 1600's, coal became the most common fuel that people in western Europe used in their homes and **industries.** Eventually, coal became the most important fuel for an invention that would change the world: the **steam engine.** A steam engine burns coal to heat water into steam.

In A.D. 60, an Egyptian scientist named Hero invented the first steam engine. The engine used steam from a kettle to turn a small, hollow globe. However, this steam engine was not particularly useful.

In 1698, an Englishman named Thomas Savery invented the first steam-driven pump to drain water out of **mines.** This steam engine did not work in the same way as modern steam engines, however. Steam is a gas that takes up more room than liquid water. Savery's engine worked by filling a space with steam. When the steam in this space was cooled, it shrank back into water, causing low air pressure. This low air pressure sucked up water out of the mines.

It was not until 1769 that a Scottish **engineer** named James Watt invented the first modern steam engine. In this engine, burning coal heats water into steam. This steam creates high pressure that moves mechanical parts in a machine. A single steam engine had the strength of many horses, without requiring the food and upkeep needed to keep horses alive.

The power provided by a steam engine depends largely on the pressure of its steam. Watt and other inventors didn't use high-pressure steam because they were afraid it might make the engine explode. In fact, Watt's engine produced steam pressure that was only slightly higher than the ordinary pressure of air. This relatively low pressure greatly limited the power of early steam engines. Eventually, steam engines ran at pressures hundreds of times higher.

Before long, people were powering more than just factories with steam engines. Steam engines came to drive **locomotives,** making it much cheaper and faster to move heavy loads across long distances. They were also used to move ships, freeing them from sails driven by wind. Steam engines powered by coal unleashed industry, leading to the **Industrial Revolution.**

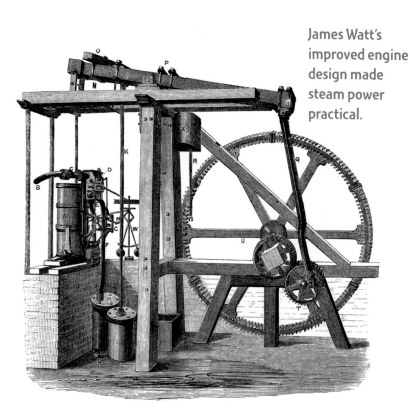

James Watt's improved engine design made steam power practical.

## James Watt

(1736–1819) was a Scottish engineer whose steam engine designs led to the development of the modern steam engine. The son of a shopkeeper and carpenter, Watt was sent off to London, England, to learn how to make machine parts. In 1763, Watt was trying to repair a steam-driven pump when he decided there must be a way to build a better steam engine. Over the next 27 years, until his retirement in 1800, Watt continued to improve steam engines. The power unit the watt was named in his honor.

# Electricity and Magnetism

**By the early 1900's, power companies used massive electric generators to provide electric power to homes and businesses.**

Thanks to the development of the **steam engine,** the **Industrial Revolution** began in Britain in the late 1700's and early 1800's. It soon spread to other parts of the world. Before this time, almost all manufacturing was done by hand. Most people lived in the countryside and worked at home, although some people had jobs in small workshops.

Once people had the technology to construct powerful steam engines, business owners could build large factories. In these factories, many people could work together to produce huge quantities of goods. More and more people left the countryside to find work in the new factories. As factories grew, cities grew along with them. This time period of rapid industrial growth forever changed the ways that people work and live.

People invented new machines to make factories bigger and better. Banks and individuals poured money into the new technology. In this new age of discovery, people began to investigate another potential source of power: electricity.

People had long known about electricity, but they did not understand what it was or how they could control it. The ancient Greeks experimented with static electricity thousands of years ago. Benjamin Franklin studied electricity in the mid-1700's. Franklin famously flew a kite during a thunderstorm until it was struck by lightning. This experiment helped prove that lightning is made of electricity.

In the 1820's, a Danish scientist named Hans C. Oersted did experiments that showed there was a connection between electricity and **magnetism.** Magnetism is the force that draws metal toward a magnet. In 1831, English scientist Michael Faraday and American scientist Joseph Henry, working independently of each other, discovered that moving a magnet near a coil of wire causes an **electric current** to flow through the wire. As the strength of the **magnetic field** changed, the strength of the electric current changed, too.

This work opened up a new world of possibility. In 1837, the American inventor Samuel F. B. Morse invented the first **telegraph.** The telegraph allowed people to send simple messages over electrical wires. For the first time, people could communicate instantaneously over long distances.

Around 30 years later, the Scottish scientist James Clerk Maxwell showed that waves moving through electric and magnetic fields move at the speed of light. He called these waves **electromagnetic waves** and suggested that visible light is made up of such waves. In the 1880's, scientists confirmed that he was correct. Today, scientists know that **radio waves, microwaves,** and **X rays** are all electromagnetic waves, too.

People began to generate electricity to provide power for homes and businesses in the late 1800's. Soon, electric power was used for countless machines, without the need for a steam engine in each machine. Today, most of the machines we use every day, from computers to washing machines, are powered by electricity.

## A CLOSER LOOK

The Industrial Revolution was a major turning point in world history. Before it began, fewer than 10 percent of the people in Europe lived in cities. By the 1850's, more than half of the people in England had followed the promise of work to live in cities. The rest of western Europe and the United States followed this trend. The rapid growth of these cities caused problems that people still struggle with today. Cities were dirty, diseased, **polluted**, and overcrowded. Work in factories was often dangerous and paid low wages. Improving these conditions took many years and itself produced many new **industries.**

# The Petroleum Industry

In 1901, the Spindletop oil field in eastern Texas first opened. The well produced a great amount of oil without pumping.

By the mid-1850's, the **Industrial Revolution** was well underway in Europe and the United States. Most factories were powered by coal, and people were starting to understand how to use electric power. Still, people continued to search for new sources of power. One of the most promising sources was **petroleum.**

Petroleum, often called oil or crude oil, is normally found in certain kinds of rocks far beneath the surface of the earth. Occasionally, oil seeps up through layers of rock to the surface. In fact, the word *petroleum* comes from Greek and Latin words that mean "rock oil." People have used small amounts of petroleum for thousands of years. People used this oil to make construction materials, **adhesives,** lubricants, ointments, and lamp fuel.

Many lamps in the early 1800's burned whale oil, which was expensive. Soon, people started burning a liquid called kerosene that came from crude oil. Kerosene was relatively cheap, and it produced strong light. As the demand for kerosene increased, people looked for better sources of oil than the few places where it seeped up out of the ground.

In 1859, "Colonel" Edwin L. Drake drilled the first oil well in Pennsylvania. That year, the United States produced around 2,000 barrels of oil. Over the next few decades, people discovered oil in California, New York, Texas, and other states. In just 40 years, U.S. oil production surged to 64 million barrels.

Around this time, people began to use less kerosene because electric light bulbs were quickly replacing lamps.

However, the invention of the automobile caused demand for petroleum to grow rapidly. **Steam engines** were not practical for automobiles, so coal was not a good source of fuel. Instead, most automobiles were powered by engines that burned gasoline, which comes from petroleum.

As automobiles became popular, the petroleum **industry** sent scientists around the world to find new sources of petroleum. Today, about two-thirds of the world's energy comes from petroleum. People around the world burn through about 84 million barrels of petroleum a day. In the United States alone, people use about 24 million barrels of petroleum each day.

**Much of the oil that people use today comes from the Middle East.**

Oil takes millions of years to form, and there are limited supplies. When petroleum is spilled, it can cause great damage to the natural environment. Burning petroleum can cause other environmental problems. Today, many people around the world are searching for new sources of power. Whole new industries are helping people use less petroleum.

**Most cars burn gasoline, which is made from oil.**

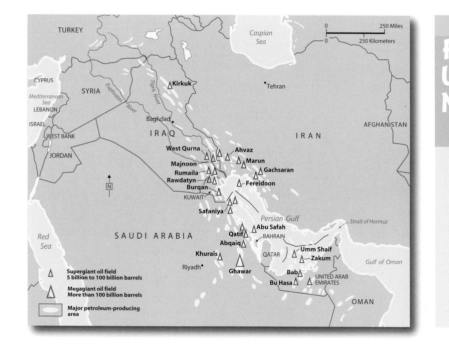

# Steel

Workers make steel at a factory in 1937.

Iron is a cheap, plentiful metal that people have valued for thousands of years. Iron is also extremely strong and durable. As early as 4000 B.C., people had begun to use iron to make weapons and tools.

Iron is plentiful, but almost all iron in the earth is mixed with substances that make it less useful. For example, when iron is exposed to air and water, it quickly rusts. Iron **ore** is rock that contains iron mixed with other substances. To get pure iron out of iron ore, people must crush the rock and melt out the iron.

Over thousands of years, people struggled to build fires that were hot enough to fully melt iron and remove unwanted substances. Ironmakers soon learned that blowing air into a furnace (enclosed chamber in which heat is produced) made the fire hotter. As people invented furnaces that produced higher heat, they were able to make more iron of a higher quality.

By the time the **Industrial Revolution** arrived, factories were making large amounts of iron. For example, American factories alone were producing around 30,000 tons (27,000 metric tons) of iron each year by the late 1700's.

As useful as iron was, steel was even better. Steel is iron that is mixed with small amounts of **carbon** and other substances. Steel weighs less than pure iron, but it is much stronger.

Since around 300 B.C., people have known how to make small amounts of steel. However, steel was extremely difficult and expensive for early people to make. If steel manufacturing was to become an **industry,** people would have to invent new, better ways to make steel.

It was not until the 1850's that a British inventor named Henry Bessemer found a way to make large amounts of steel at low cost. Soon,

The hulls of most ships are made from steel.

steel production increased dramatically. In 1880, U.S. companies produced about 1.4 million tons (1.3 million metric tons) of steel. By 1910, production had increased to 24 million tons (22 million metric tons). Even better methods of making steel have helped production grow steadily since then.

Today, almost all the iron that is **mined** around the world is eventually turned into steel. Steel is used to build **skyscrapers.** It is used to make railroad tracks and the trains that ride upon them. Cars, trucks, and ships are all made of steel. Even the simple paper clip is made of steel. Today, the worldwide steel industry produces more than 1 billion tons (910 million metric tons) of this invaluable metal each year.

## A CLOSER LOOK

As early as 4000 B.C., people started using iron to make tools and weapons. They collected this iron from meteorites, which are stones that fall from space. Pure iron is common in space but rare on Earth. In fact, in several ancient languages, the words for *iron* meant "stone from heaven" or "star metal." By 1400 B.C., ancient people living in what is now Turkey had learned how to use furnaces to make their own iron tools and weapons. Learning how to make iron tools and weapons was such an important advance that people often call this time period the Iron Age.

# ▶ Refrigeration

**People once cut blocks of ice from lakes and rivers to keep food cold.**

tance. People in crowded cities could not grow their own food.

As cities grew, ever more food had to be brought in from the countryside. If the food spoiled before people could eat it, the people would go hungry. Sometimes, food goes bad before its smell or appearance changes. If people eat this food, they can become terribly ill or even die.

In the early 1800's, people started canning foods to preserve them. They

**Early refrigerators were often called ice boxes.**

Until recently, most people around the world grew their own food. People have long needed ways to store and save some of that food so it could last through winter. People discovered that grains, nuts, and fruit can be dried in the sun. People learned to smoke fish and meat over open fires to keep the flesh from spoiling. People also learned that salting meat could **preserve** it for months.

As people moved from farms to cities during the **Industrial Revolution,** preserving food took on new impor-

packed food into glass jars, covered these jars tightly with a lid, and then heated the filled jars in boiling water. This method killed most of the **germs** that spoil food, allowing food to be kept for months or even years. People also used ice to keep food cold, because cold slows the growth of germs. People cut large blocks of ice from rivers and lakes during winter, packing it in sawdust to slow melting. However, this ice lasted for only a limited time once summer arrived.

In 1851, an American doctor named John Gorrie invented a machine that could make ice. Gorrie used his machine to help people suffering fevers. Other people began using this technology to refrigerate foods while they were stored and shipped.

Soon, many inventors began to search for better methods of **refrigeration.** In the 1870's, a German **engineer** named Carl von Linde began to build and sell refrigerators that reliably kept food at temperatures between 32 °F and 40 °F (0 °C and 4 °C). These refrigerators changed how long people could store such foods as meat, which can spoil in a single day if it is not kept cool.

Today, there are many different kinds of refrigerators. These machines keep foods fresh, no matter how hot the weather outside. The invention of refrigeration gave people many new food

Refrigerated trucks keep treats cold on even the hottest summer days.

options. Food can be loaded into refrigerated containers and shipped across the country. Refrigerated containers on ships can even carry food across the oceans. Refrigeration helped ensure that people in the cities would always have good food to eat, allowing the Industrial Revolution to grow.

**FUN FACT**

If you wet your hands and quickly wave them back and forth, they will become cool. This is because when water **evaporates** off your skin, it turns from liquid to gas. As it changes to gas, the water absorbs the heat around it, cooling your skin. The same effect explains why people sweat. Fans keep people cool by moving air over the skin, which helps sweat evaporate. Some kinds of refrigeration work in the same way.

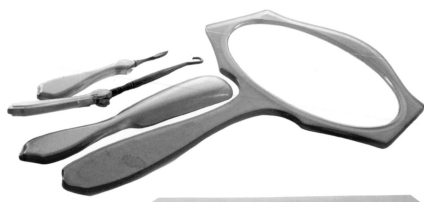

# ▶ Plastics

Bakelite plastic was used in a variety of products.

P lastics are manufactured materials that can be shaped into almost any form. They are one of the most useful materials ever created. Today, our homes, schools, and businesses are filled with plastic products.

Plastics can be as rigid as steel or as soft as cotton. Plastics help protect our bodies during automobile accidents. Plastics are so important today that it's hard to imagine life without them.

Yet, plastics are another kind of material that was invented during the **Industrial Revolution.**

For thousands of years, people used natural gums and resins (sticky substances from certain plants or trees) that somewhat resemble plastics. For example, the ancient Greeks and **Romans** made ornaments out of amber, which is fossilized tree resin. In the **Middle Ages,** people in Europe coated wooden objects with shellac to protect them from water. Shellac is made from a substance produced by a certain kind of insect.

As the Industrial Revolution grew, factories needed ever growing amounts of resin. Factories shaped resin into such products as brush handles, knobs, electrical **insulation,** and **phonograph records.** Unfortunately, natural resins were expensive, and the finished products were often brittle and easily damaged.

In the late 1860's, a New York printer named John W. Hyatt invented a substance called celluloid. He was trying to make billiard balls out of something other than ivory, which was

**Plastic containers are useful for storing food and other items.**

In the years that followed, scientists invented hundreds of different kinds of plastics. Such plastics as acrylic, nylon, and vinyl are used to make clothing. Plastics are used to make garden hoses, raincoats, electric plugs, plumbing fixtures, computer disks, and televisions. Plastics are cheaper to make, weigh less, and often last longer than paper, wood, and stone.

expensive and scarce. Hyatt mixed a material in plants called cellulose with other chemicals to make celluloid. Celluloid was hard and stiff, but it could be heated and shaped into a variety of forms. The problem with celluloid was that it easily caught fire.

Finally, in the early 1900's, a New York chemist named Leo Baekeland invented the first true plastic. Baekeland mixed together chemicals found in **petroleum** to make a plastic he called Bakelite. Soon, Bakelite was used to make such products as telephones and pot handles. It is still used today to make electrical and automobile parts.

**A CLOSER LOOK**

Though plastic is one of the most useful materials ever invented, it also **pollutes** the natural environment. Plastics are made from petroleum, and they do not break down easily. In a **landfill**, a plastic milk jug can take a million years to break down. Billions of pieces of plastic litter the world's oceans, killing untold numbers of sea creatures every year. Americans throw away 100 billion plastic bags every year.

# Steam Turbines

**The *Turbinia* was the first ship to be powered by a steam turbine.**

The development of the **steam engine** in the late 1700's revolutionized **industry.** As the **Industrial Revolution** gained speed in the 1800's, steam engines provided much of the power that drove the new factories.

In the early 1900's, people started building a new kind of steam engine called a steam **turbine.** A steam turbine is essentially an enclosed wheel with blades all around its surface. As steam presses against the blades, the wheel spins on an **axle.**

Steam turbines were built around the ancient idea of the **water wheel,** which is the oldest known turbine. In a water wheel, the force of water causes the

wheel to turn, spinning it on an axle. The axle turns **gears** in a simple motor that does work, such as grinding grain. In early water wheels, some of the moving water escaped around the edges of the wheel's blades, reducing power. During the 1800's, people started building the first closed wheels, which did not allow water to escape around the edges of the wheel.

In 1884, an English inventor named Charles A. Parsons used a closed-wheel turbine in a steam engine. This engine worked by heating water into steam in a large boiler, just as steam is created in a normal steam engine. Then, at very high pressures, the steam enters a turbine, causing the turbine wheel to spin rapidly. The spinning steam turbine could drive much more powerful motors than a water wheel.

In 1897, Parsons became the first person to use a steam turbine to power a ship. Appropriately, he named this ship the *Turbinia.* Steam turbines were smaller and lighter than steam engines. They also provided much more power.

By the early 1900's, electric companies were using steam turbines to create

Steam turbines are used to produce electricity at power plants. Superheated steam turns the turbine, which runs a generator. The generator has a rotating **electromagnet** called a rotor and a stationary part called a stator. A separate generator called an exciter powers the rotor, creating a **magnetic field** that produces an electric charge in the stator. The charge is transmitted as electricity and transferred to a transformer, a device that increases the strength of the electrical force.

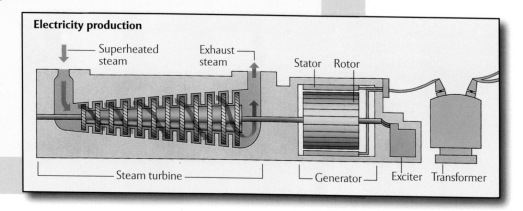

**Electricity production**

Superheated steam — Exhaust steam — Stator — Rotor

Steam turbine — Generator — Exciter — Transformer

electric power. Coal or another fuel heated water into steam, driving the steam turbine. The steam turbine powered a **generator.**

The generator created electric power based on Michael Faraday's and Joseph Henry's discovery that moving a magnet near a coil of wire causes an **electric current** to flow through the wire. Most **power plants** still use steam turbines to create electric power.

Today, huge steam turbines power giant ships and massive machines. Steam turbines turning electric generators can create nearly 750 million watts of power, enough to power about 750,000 homes.

Steam turbines drive ships and generate electricity.

An assembly line enables workers to build cars more quickly.

Generally, the longer it takes to make something, the more it costs. Factories manufacture products much more quickly than people can on their own. With each passing year of the **Industrial Revolution,** people looked for faster and better ways to do the work.

In 1903, an American businessman named Henry Ford started the Ford Motor Company. His first cars were hand-built and relatively expensive. Ford decided to build a simple, sturdy car that ordinary people could afford. In 1908, he introduced a relatively inexpensive car called the Model T, which sold for about $850. However, this car was still too expensive for most people to buy. Ford searched for ways to lower the cost of making the Model T so he could lower its price for customers even further.

In most car factories of that period, a small group of people worked together to build an entire car. Each person in the group did many different tasks, which made the work complicated. The average time to build a car was 12.5 hours.

Ford revolutionized **industry** by building conveyer belts that would carry car parts to people on a long **assembly line.** One person would do only one task, such as tighten a bolt. The person would do this task over and over again as part after part moved along the belt. At the end of the assembly line, the car was finished.

Ford's assembly line cut the time needed to build a car down to only 1.5 hours per car. As the price to build a car plummeted, Ford lowered the cost

Modern factories use assembly lines to build most products.

of the Model T. Cars that cost $850 in 1908 cost only $550 in 1913, $440 in 1915, and $290 in 1924. For the first time, cars became affordable to the average American family.

Ford also changed the way he paid the people in his factories. Anyone who was older than 22 received at least $5 per day. This amount was about twice as much as other companies were paying. Ford also cut down the number of hours that his employees worked, from nine hours a day to eight. These improved conditions helped attract the smartest, best workers to Ford's factories.

The assembly line quickly spread to factories making all sorts of products. It allowed more goods to be produced more quickly at lower cost.

## Henry Ford

Henry Ford (1863–1947) is famous for introducing the assembly line to his automobile company. Ford was born on a farm in Michigan. He was interested in automobiles from a young age. He built his first engine in 1893 and his first whole car in 1896. He was also active in politics. During World War I (1914-1918), he paid travel expenses to Europe for himself and a large group of people trying to stop the war. He also ran for the U.S. Senate in 1918. Both of those efforts failed.

# ▶ Adhesives

**People once used glues made from the bodies of fish.**

**A**dhesives, sometimes called glues, are a kind of substance that people have used for thousands of years. Adhesives are extremely useful because they make different materials stick together. For as long as people have made pottery and other fragile (breakable) objects, they have accidentally dropped those objects and caused them to shatter. Adhesives allowed people to repair damaged objects. Adhesives are also useful for manufacturing many goods. For example, the pages in this book are bound together by adhesive along the spine of the book.

People have probably used adhesives for longer than they have known how to write down words. Ancient people made glue out of such materials as egg yolks, blood, bones, hooves, beeswax, milk, tree sap, vegetables, and grains. However, none of these adhesives were especially strong or long-lasting.

In the mid-1700's, England awarded the first **patent** for a glue made from the bodies of fish. Unfortunately, fish glue loses its strength if it is not used within two years of when it is made. People still needed better glues.

When scientists started experimenting with different chemicals in the 1930's and 1940's, they began to invent completely new kinds of adhesives. Around 1940, an American **engineer** named Paul Cope created a hot glue made of melted plastic. The melted plastic hardened as it cooled, binding materials together. Although hot glue does not hold materials together tightly, people still use it today in crafts. Hot glue sticks and hot glue guns, which are used to melt the glue, are available at hardware stores.

Perhaps the greatest invention in the history of adhesives came in 1942. In that year, a researcher named Dr. Harry Coover created a substance called cyanoacrylate. Coover was experimenting with different chemicals in an effort to make clear plastic parts for guns. He couldn't use the cyanoacrylate he created because it was too sticky. A few years later, Coover was searching for something that could glue together airplane parts. He remembered cyanoacrylate and tested it. It worked perfectly. People still use cyanoacrylate, which is sold as a product called Superglue.

Since the 1940's, scientists have invented many other adhesives. Today, factories use adhesives to manufacture a variety of products. Automobile and airplane parts are held together with super-strong adhesives. The furniture **industry** glues wood together to make furniture. Many furniture factories build items out of particle board, which is made of compressed

glue and wood chips. Sandpaper is made by gluing scratchy sand to a paper backing. Glue is used to stiffen cloth in the fabric industry. People have even invented special kinds of adhesive that can hold together the edges of torn flesh while it heals.

Adhesives hold the parts of a violin together.

# ► Transistors

Transistors made such electronics as radios lighter and more reliable.

In the late 1800's, a number of different people invented the technology that made radio communication possible. Radios work by using antennas to pick up **electromagnetic waves** passing through the atmosphere. These waves create weak **electric currents** in the antenna. The radio turns these currents into sound.

The first radios were bulky machines that hardly resemble modern radios. One of the reasons why early radios were so big is that they used **vacuum tubes** to control the signals picked up by the antenna. Vacuum tubes resemble light bulbs but produce no light. They were large, fragile, unreliable, and expensive to produce. They consumed large quantities of electric power and gave off much heat. The future of **electronics** was limited as long as the devices used vacuum tubes.

In 1947, three American scientists named John Bardeen, Walter H. Brattain, and William Shockley invented the **transistor.** Like vacuum tubes, transistors work by switching electric current on and off. They also strengthen the power in the electric current.

Though they work in similar ways, transistors offer many advantages over vacuum tubes. Transistors are much smaller and cheaper to build. They are more durable and reliable. They don't require nearly as much electric power to run, and they give off much less heat.

People first began building transistors into small "pocket" radios and hearing aids in the 1950's. Over time, people started putting transistors into almost every electrical device.

As scientists discovered ways to make transistors smaller, transistors became even more useful. People learned that they could build computers by putting many transistors together on a single chip. Early computers were the size of entire buildings because of all the vacuum tubes they needed. When these tubes were replaced by transistors, the computers shrank in size while becoming more reliable and powerful.

As transistors have improved, computer chips have become smaller, lighter, and more powerful. Today, transistors may be only 45 nanometers across. A nanometer is a billionth of a meter (1/25,400,000 inch). Such transistors are so small that it would take more than 2,000 of them just to equal the width of an average human hair!

Modern transistors are so small that a computer chip the size of a fingernail can hold hundreds of millions of transistors. Incredibly, scientists are hard at work on transistors that are smaller still.

Today, computer chips are in thousands of products, from **cellular telephones** to automobiles to toaster ovens. The computers that people carry in their hands are more powerful than the computers that were the size of a building just a few decades ago. None of this would be possible without the transistor.

Today, computer chips are loaded with millions of transistors.

# ► Lasers

Laser scanners are used to read the bar code on goods.

Lasers produce strong beams of light that can be used to drill through extremely hard surfaces, such as sheet iron.

After World War II (1939-1945), inventions in **electronics** became important to almost every **industry.** The invention of the **transistor** eventually led to handheld computers and **cellular telephones.** Soon, scientists invented another new technology that would forever change a wide variety of industries. This technology was the **laser.**

In 1917, the famous German-born physicist Albert Einstein described how **atoms** can give off various forms of **electromagnetic waves,** including visible light. In 1954, an American scientist named Charles H. Townes designed a device that used Einstein's insight to generate a tightly focused, extremely intense beam of **microwaves.** Microwaves are a type of electromagnetic wave. Townes called his device a maser.

After several years of research, Townes began working with his brother-in-law, Arthur Schawlow, to create a new device. This device would resemble a maser but would achieve the same tightly focused, intense beam with visible light. They called this device a laser.

Townes and his team hoped to use lasers to send signals through space. They also thought that lasers might one day be used to cut and drill through hard surfaces. Working with a graduate student named Gordon Gould, they made great progress toward building such a laser.

However, it was another scientist who first succeeded in constructing a true laser. In 1960, Theodore H. Maiman used a photographer's flash bulb to fire bright flashes of light at a special ruby crystal. Maiman's laser produced red pulses of light that were high in energy.

Additional laser developments soon followed. As lasers became more powerful, people were still not completely sure how they could be used. In time, people realized that lasers were one of the most useful technologies ever invented. As Townes's team had hoped, lasers can be used to send signals through space. For example, scientists have fired lasers at the moon, reflecting them back to Earth. Lasers can also be used to drill through hard surfaces.

Lasers are used in medicine and many other industries.

Today, lasers are used in a variety of industries. Eye surgeons use lasers to correct people's vision and to repair a part of the eye called the retina. In the 1970's, people built laser scanners at grocery store checkout lines. These scanners allow computers to check the price of products automatically. Both CD's and DVD's would be impossible without lasers, because lasers both burn and read the information on these discs. Lasers are crucial to the communications industry, sending huge amounts of information over special glass **optical fibers.**

Charles H. Townes helped invent the laser.

# ▶ Robotics

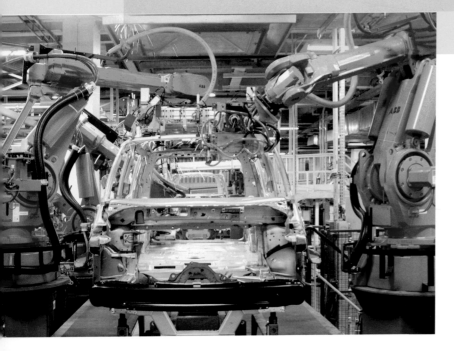

**Robots have replaced people on many assembly lines.**

The idea of robots has been around for a long time. In the early 1920's and 1930's, people built **automated** steering systems into planes and ships to help human pilots and captains avoid danger. During World War II (1939-1945), **radar** was linked to antiaircraft guns. Such guns could automatically detect enemy planes, aim, and fire.

In 1961, people installed the first robot to work in an automobile factory. A computer controlled its motions. As computer technology continued to improve, more and more robots were installed in factories. Today, some factories hardly employ people at all.

Robots offer many advantages. They never become tired or bored. Also, robots can work in dangerous conditions but never become injured. For example, robots are used for repairing underwater pipelines at dangerously high pressures. Automobiles are painted by robots using spray paint that would harm people.

Some robots perform work that is too difficult for people to do. For example, high-speed military aircraft sometimes fly just above the trees to avoid

The **assembly line** brought many improvements to **industries** that manufacture goods. Unfortunately, it also brought problems. By dividing the work into simple, repetitive tasks, the assembly line made some factory work extremely boring for people to do. Also, making the same movement over and over again for long periods of time—such as tightening a single bolt hundreds of times each day over many years—can cause people to suffer injuries.

To solve these problems, people started experimenting with the idea of using robots to perform certain tasks. A robot is a mechanical device that operates automatically.

Robotic arms wired into the brain can replace missing limbs.

detection by enemy radar. These aircraft use robotic systems that can react much faster than a pilot can.

Robots vary in design and size, but few resemble the humanlike machines that appear in works of science fiction. Most are stationary structures with a single arm capable of lifting objects and using tools.

Today, robots have left the factory and entered the home. A popular robot called the Roomba is a robotic vacuum cleaner that automatically cleans carpets and then returns to its base. Other robots can mow the lawn. There are even robotic pets.

Robots have become important to the military, as well. The U.S. military uses robotic aircraft that take pictures of the battlefield. These robots can even fire missiles at enemy vehicles and buildings, though humans control whether the robots fire.

Robots have also proved crucial in exploring space. All the **probes** people have sent to other planets are robots. Today, robotic rovers (exploration vehicles) are exploring the surface of Mars to investigate whether that planet was ever suitable for life. As robots continue to become more advanced, they are sure to change the world in ways that are hard to imagine today.

Spirit is a robotic rover that has explored Mars since 2004.

# ▶ Biotechnology

**People have used biotechnology to make beer since ancient times.**

**B**iotechnology is one of the newest additions to the growing list of modern **industries.** Biotechnology brings together scientific understanding of living things with modern technology to make products that are useful to people.

Biotechnology is a modern industry, but people have used simple biotechnology for thousands of years. Beer, wine, and cheese all rely on **microor-**

**ganisms** to change raw ingredients into the finished product. For example, in the case of wine, microorganisms change the sugar in grape juice into alcohol. Even though ancient people did not know how microorganisms actually did this work, they became experts at producing rich, flavorful wines.

Modern biotechnology was born with the discovery of penicillin in 1928. Penicillin is a natural substance made by a kind of mold. Penicillin revolutionized medicine because it kills the microorganisms that cause such diseases as pneumonia, rheumatic fever, and scarlet fever.

Penicillin inspired scientists to search for other natural substances that could treat disease. Scientists also developed ways to create such substances themselves. Today, the pharmaceutical (medicinal drug) industry is a large and successful area of biotechnology. Pharmaceutical companies produce thousands of drugs to treat diseases ranging from the simple flu to the most deadly forms of cancer.

Biotechnology began with the production of such foods as beer, wine, and cheese. Today, biotechnology is changing food production again. Scientists have used **genetic engineering** to create new breeds of such crops as corn, cotton, potatoes, rice, soybeans, and tomatoes. The new breeds of these crops offer various advantages. They may resist drought (a long period of dry weather) or disease. They may require fewer chemicals to help the crops grow, reducing **pollution.** Other genetically engineered crops last longer on the shelf before spoiling, while still others contain vitamins people need.

Biotechnology also includes efforts to replace fuels, such as coal and **petroleum.** These fuels pollute the environment, and their limited supplies will eventually run out. Using biotechnology, people may be able to turn grass or even microorganisms into fuel. Scientists have already created microorganisms that help to clean up oil spills.

Scientists are also using biotechnology to create new kinds of plastics that are made from plants rather than petroleum. These new plastics should break down quickly when exposed to sun and weather, instead of filling **landfills** for many years.

Biotechnology has the potential to change many industries. Biotechnology may ultimately give people ways to clean up the pollution caused by the **Industrial Revolution.** As people

continue to invent technology and create new **industries,** the only thing for certain is that the world will continue to change.

Scientists are inventing better crops and new sources of fuel.

### A CLOSER LOOK

Biotechnology has great potential, but it has also raised concerns. For example, genetically engineered crops have caused much controversy. Critics worry that such crops may be unhealthy or may spread to the wild, replacing ordinary plants. But most scientists argue that there is no solid evidence that genetically engineered crops are unsafe. Other advances have also been controversial. For example, using biotechnology, it may be possible to grow an exact copy of an adult human's body in a process called cloning. Many countries have already made such cloning illegal, though no one has successfully cloned a person so far.

# Important Dates in Industry and Manufacturing

**c. 600,000–400,000 B.C.** People learned how to use and control fire.

**c. 4000 B.C.** People started making the first iron tools.

**c. 3500 B.C.** Sumerian people were using wheels to make carts.

**c. 1500 B.C.** People in Egypt and Mesopotamia began making glass objects.

**c. 1400 B.C.** Hittite people used iron to forge tools.

**c. 500 B.C.** People invented gears.

**c. 400 B.C.** People invented pulleys.

**c. 300 B.C.** People began making steel.

**c. 100 B.C.** Ancient Romans developed the first concrete.

**A.D. 1756** John Smeaton of England rediscovered how to make concrete.

**1769** James Watt of England invented the first steam engine.

**1820's** The Danish scientist Hans C. Oersted experimented with electric power and magnets.

**1851** The American Dr. John Gorrie invented a machine that could make ice.

**1859** "Colonel" Edwin L. Drake drilled the first oil well in Pennsylvania.

**1860's** The Scottish scientist James Clerk Maxwell created a magnetic field using electric power.

**Late 1860's** The American scientist John W. Hyatt invented celluloid.

**1879** The glass light bulb was invented.

**1884** The English scientist Charles A. Parsons created a working steam turbine engine.

**Early 1900's** The American scientist Leo Baekeland invented Bakelite plastic.

**1940** The American scientist Paul Cope invented the first chemically made hot glue.

**1947** The first transistor was invented.

**1950's** People began building the first transistor radios and computers.

**1951** Charles H. Townes invented the maser.

**1960** Theodore H. Maiman created the first laser.

**1961** The first automated robot was installed in an automotive factory in the United States.

**1970** Glass fibers for communication (optical fibers) were invented in the United States.

# Glossary

**adhesive** glue, paste, or any other substance useful for sticking things together.

**assembly line** a row of workers and machines along which work is passed until the final product is made.

**atom** one of the basic units of matter.

**automated** the use of automatic controls in the operation of machinery.

**axle** a bar or shaft on which a wheel turns.

**biotechnology** the combination of scientific understanding of living things with modern technology to make products for people.

**carbon** a very common chemical element that occurs in combination with other elements in all plants and animals.

**cellular telephone** a wireless telephone that transmits and receives messages via radio signals.

**electric current** the movement or flow of electric charges.

**electromagnet** a temporary magnet formed when electric current flows through a wire or other conductor.

**electromagnetic waves** related patterns of electric and magnetic force that travel through space.

**electronics** devices that make use of electricity and transistors. Cellular telephones, computers, and televisions are all examples of electronics.

**engineer** a person who plans and builds engines, machines, roads, bridges, canals, forts, or the like.

**evaporate** to change from a liquid or solid into a vapor (gas).

**friction** a rubbing of one object against another. Friction typically creates heat.

**fulcrum** the support on which a lever turns or is supported in moving or lifting an object.

**gear** a wheel having teeth that fit into the teeth of another wheel.

**generator** a machine that changes mechanical energy into electrical energy and produces either direct or alternating current.

**genetic engineering** a group of techniques that are used to change the genes in an organism.

**germ** a microorganism that causes disease. Germs include bacteria, viruses, and protozoa.

**industry** any branch of business, trade, or manufacture.

**Industrial Revolution** a period in the late 1700's and early 1800's when the development of industries brought great change to many parts of the world.

**insulation** a material that prevents the loss or transfer of electricity, heat, or sound.

**landfill** a place where trash is buried.

**laser** a device that produces a very narrow and intense beam of coherent light.

**lever** a bar that rests on a fixed support called a fulcrum. One end of the bar transmits force and motion to the other end, much like the action of a seesaw.

**locomotive** a machine that moves trains on railroad tracks.

**magnetic field** the space around a magnet in which its power of attraction is effective.

**magnetism** the properties or qualities of a magnet; the ability to attract certain metallic objects.

**microorganism** a living creature too small to be seen without a microscope.

**microwave** a high-frequency electromagnetic wave.

**Middle Ages** the period in European history between ancient and modern times, from about the A.D. 400's through the 1400's.

**mill** a building where manufacturing is done.

**mine** (n.) a large hole or space dug in the earth to get out ores, precious stones, coal, salt, or anything valuable. (v.) to make a hole or space in the earth in order to get out ores, coal, or anything valuable.

**optical fiber** a long, thin strand of glass that carries light, allowing the transfer of information at great speeds.

**ore** a mineral or rock that contains pure metal mixed with other substances.

**patent** a government-issued document that grants an inventor exclusive rights to an invention for a limited time.

**petroleum** an oily, dark, flammable liquid found in the earth. Also called oil or crude oil.

**phonograph record** a thin disk, now usually of vinyl or other plastic, on the surface of which sound is transcribed in narrow grooves.

**pollute; pollution** to make physically impure, foul, or dirty; the ways in which human activity harms the natural environment.

**power plant** a building with machinery for generating power.

**preserve** to keep from harm or change.

**probe** a rocket, satellite, or other unmanned spacecraft carrying scientific instruments.

**pulley** a wheel with a rope over it, such that the wheel changes the direction of force when the rope is pulled.

**radar** an instrument for determining the distance, direction, and speed of unseen objects by the reflection of radio waves.

**radio wave** an electromagnetic wave within the radio frequencies.

**refrigeration** the act or process of cooling or keeping cold.

**Renaissance** a great revival of art and learning in Europe from A.D. 1300-1500.

**Roman** of or having to do with ancient Rome or its people. The Roman Empire controlled most of Europe and the Middle East from 27 B.C. to A.D. 476.

**skyscraper** an extremely tall building.

**steam engine** an engine that is operated by the energy of expanding steam.

**telegraph** an instrument used to send messages by means of wires and electric current.

**transistor** an electrical device that controls the flow and can boost the power of electric current.

**turbine** a device with a rotor turned by a moving fluid, such as water, steam, gas, or wind.

**vacuum tube** a sealed glass tube or bulb from which almost all the air has been removed, used to control the flow of electric current.

**water wheel** a wheel that is turned by water and uses that power to drive machinery, such as that of a mill.

**windmill** a machine that is operated by wind power which can be used to provide power to pump water, grind grain, or generate electric power.

**X rays** invisible rays that can be used to produce pictures of bones and other body structures.

# ▶ Additional Resources

## Books:

- *Amazing Leonardo da Vinci Inventions You Can Build Yourself* by Maxine Anderson (Nomad Press, 2006).

- *Great Inventions: The Illustrated Science Encyclopedia* by Peter Harrison, Chris Oxlade, and Stephen Bennington (Southwater Publishing, 2001).

- *Great Inventions of the 20th Century* by Peter Jedicke (Chelsea House Publications, 2007).

- *Inventions* by Valerie Wyatt (Kids Can Press, 2003).

- *Smokestacks and Spinning Jennys: Industrial Revolution* by Sean Price (Raintree, 2007).

- *So You Want to Be an Inventor?* by Judith St. George (Philomel Books, 2002).

- *What a Great Idea! Inventions that Changed the World* by Stephen M. Tomecek (Scholastic, 2003).

## Web Sites:

- Exploring Leonardo - Museum of Science, Boston
  http://www.mos.org/sln/Leonardo
  Focusing on Leonardo da Vinci, this Web site provides information for teachers and students in grades 4-8. Areas covered include a section on the elements of machines (the lever, gears) and a discussion of perspective.

- Henry Ford
  http://www.invent.org/hall_of_fame/60.html
  Information from the National Inventors Hall of Fame about pioneering automotive engineer Henry Ford.

- Thomas Alva Edison
  http://www.invent.org/hall_of_fame/50.html
  A Web site with biographical information on Thomas Edison.

- National Inventors Hall of Fame
  http://www.invent.org/index.asp
  Information on inventions and inventors from the National Inventors Hall of Fame.

- Encyclopedia Smithsonian: Engineering, Industry, and Invention
  http://www.si.edu/Encyclopedia_SI/science_and_technology/EngineeringandIndustry_Technology.htm
  Includes links to information on science and technology throughout the history of the United States.

- The Lemelson Center for the Study of Invention and Innovation
  http://invention.smithsonian.org/home
  Features information on inventions and their creators, podcasts and videos from scientists, and at-home experiments for students.

# Index